DAYS OF TRAGEDY

The Assassination of a President:
JOHN F. KENNEDY

Written by:
Sue L. Hamilton

Published by Abdo & Daughters, 6537 Cecilia Circle, Bloomington, Minnesota 55435

Library bound edition distributed by Rockbottom Books, Pentagon Tower, P.O. Box 36036, Minneapolis, Minnesota 55435

Library of Congress Number: 89-084903   ISBN: 0-939179-55-5

Cover Photo by: Bettmann Newsphotos
Inside Photos by: Bettmann Newsphotos

Edited by: John C. Hamilton

FORWARD

November 22, 1963   12:30 p.m.

Blast . . . Blast! Blast! President John F. Kennedy lurched forward in his seat, his hands clutching his throat. "Get down!" shouted the Secret Servicemen to the crowd of confused Texans.

Standing on the running boards of the president's 1961 Lincoln Continental limousine, one agent shouted to the driver, "Get us out of here! The president's hit!"

The happy shouts and whistles that 5.6 seconds before had reached Lee Harvey Oswald's ears were now replaced by the terrified cries of the witnesses to his crime. "I've done it!" thought the 24-year-old murderer excitedly, as he slowly lowered his 6.5mm 1938 Mannlicher-Carcano rifle.

Turning from the eastern-most window of the Texas School Book Depository building, he lowered his deadly weapon and wedged it between two boxes of books. Quickly, he hurried down two flights of stairs to hide in the lunchroom. Then, at his first chance, he escaped to the street below.

Utter confusion met Oswald's eyes as police and Secret Servicemen tried to help the frightened people on Elm Street. Seemingly unnoticed, the 24-year-old ex-resident of Russia hurried down the street to the nearest waiting bus. As he climbed in, his two words to the bus driver hardly seemed fitting for the man who had just killed the president: "Transfer please."

CHAPTER 1 — THE KILLER

Lee Harvey Oswald was an odd young man with a strange history. He was born in New Orleans, Louisiana on October 18, 1939, two months after his father died of a sudden heart attack. At the age of 17 he joined the U.S. Marines. While in the service, he learned how to shoot rifles, and was given a marksman's medal. However, he often challenged his superior officers, and landed himself in jail more than once. He never made any close friends, and preferred studying Russian government to a game of football.

When his mother had a small injury, he used this excuse to get out of the service. He went home to Fort Worth, Texas to take care of her. However, he stayed with her only three days, and in September of 1959, he left for Russia.

On October 17, he tried to become a Soviet citizen. The Russians told him to leave. To prove he meant business, Oswald cut his wrists, trying to kill himself rather than return to the United States. He was found and rushed to a hospital. The Soviets decided to let him stay, but he could not become a citizen.

Oswald met Marina, the daughter of a Russian KGB colonel, in March of 1961. Within a month, they were married. On February 15, of the following year, their first daughter, June Lee, was born. Oswald had a family, job, and home in Russia. However, he was finding that life in the USSR was not what he thought it would be. He had none of the freedoms he had in the United States. He especially missed being able to target shoot, and finally decided to get permission from the Soviets to leave.

On June 13, 1962, the Oswalds returned to the U.S., arriving in Dallas. Oswald had a tough time keeping jobs. He often argued with Marina. Things were not going well. Oswald blamed everyone but himself for his bad luck. He hated how the United States was run. He hated his life. And, strangely enough, he hated anyone who hated Russia.

Ex-Major General Edwin Walker was one of the most outspoken anti-Russian and anti-Communist people living in Dallas. Oswald decided to kill him. On April 10, 1963, at about 9:00 p.m., Oswald balanced his gun on the top of Walker's car parked outside, and aimed through a nearby window. The room was brightly lit, and Oswald could see the Major General sitting at his desk. An easy shot. Oswald squeezed the trigger. He saw his target jump! Certain that he had got him, Oswald raced off. However, Walker was not hit. The telescope on Oswald's rifle was off, and his sure shot had missed. The would-be killer did not find out until later. However, he learned a valuable lesson: one shot was not enough.

CHAPTER 2 — OSWALD'S PLAN

Marina had just given birth to their second daughter, Audrey Marina Rachel on October 19, 1963. Three days earlier, Oswald had gotten a job at the Texas School Book Depository. His wife and children stayed with a friend, Mrs. Ruth Paine, who lived in a house in Irving, Texas, just outside of Dallas. Oswald rented a room in town. Oswald rode out to visit his family on weekends, getting a ride from a neighbor boy who also worked at the Depository, Wesley Frazier.

Oswald had grown more and more angry. He wanted to do something to prove that he was somebody special. Somebody everyone would remember. He wanted to be respected and feared. He made no secret that he was a Communist. That brought him to the attention of the FBI and CIA, something Oswald did not want. He often felt that they were "after him." Although both security groups did have files on Oswald, as far as they knew he was no threat to anyone. Tragically, they were dead wrong.

On Thursday, November 21, Oswald entered the lunchroom at work and began reading the *Dallas Herald*. The top story reported that President Kennedy would be in Dallas tomorrow. The newspaper showed the route the president's car would take. Oswald saw that it would go right by the Texas School Book Depository. President Kennedy would be less than 100 feet away from him. Oswald went back to work, his mind filled with plans. He would go out to see his family and pick up his rifle that night.

That afternoon, Oswald stopped Wesley Frazier. "Can I get a ride with you out to Irving tonight?" he asked in his usual short manner.

"Sure, Lee," said Frazier, somewhat puzzled. "But I thought you usually go out on Friday."

"I want to see Marina and the kids," said Oswald. "And I have to pick up some curtain rods for my room," he lied, setting up a way for him to get his rifle back without further questions.

"Sure, Lee," answered Frazier. "Any time."

CHAPTER 3 —
THE LAST MORNING

President John F. Kennedy ("Jack" to his friends) was pleased that Friday morning, November 22, 1963. In the last few days, he and Mrs. Kennedy had been to San Antonio, Houston, and now Fort Worth. In all these cities, the crowds that had come to see him and his wife were always bigger than expected. People loved to see the pretty First Lady, and this was her first "real" political trip. Kennedy was campaigning for reelection, and Texas was an important state to win.

Vice President Lyndon Johnson and his wife, Lady Bird, were also on the trip. It was a tough schedule, flying city-to-city. Activities began early in the morning and lasted until late in the evening. It was hard work, but that's what kept the president in office. Besides, after this, the country's top two couples were looking forward to a few days of fun at the Johnson's ranch.

At 7:30 that morning, President Kennedy drew back the curtains of Suite 850 in Fort Worth's Hotel Texas. He was already shaved and dressed in his grey-blue suit, ready for the day. Mrs. Kennedy was also up.

"Look at that crowd," he said to her. "Just look." Mrs. Kennedy peered out. It was raining, but that hadn't stopped over 2,000 Texans from gathering in the parking lot to hear the president speak. It was a good sign.

The president would give two speeches, one to the crowd outside, and one to the Fort Worth Chamber of Commerce, before going out to the airport, where his jet, *Air Force One*, waited. AF-1 held the President and Mrs. Kennedy, Texas' Governor John Connally, his wife Nellie, Senator Ralph Yarborough, and Kennedy's own assistants and security people. Aboard *Air Force Two* were Vice President and Mrs. Johnson and their staff. Reporters and photographers were on a third jet. The three jets would fly the short 33 miles to Dallas' Love Field.

Meanwhile, in a house outside Dallas, Oswald finished his morning coffee. He had left his wedding ring and $170 for Marina on the table next to the bed. Everyone was still asleep as the thin young man walked out to the garage. He found his rifle and took it apart. Carefully, he wrapped the two pieces in a long bag that he had made out of brown paper.

With his deadly package held tightly, Oswald walked through the gloomy rain to Frazier's house. He reached the teen-ager's 1954 Chevrolet and placed the package in the back seat. Instead of going up to get Wes, he waited alone in the garage for his driver to come out.

It didn't take long. The two got in and Frazier started the old car. Glancing at the back seat, he asked, "What's in the package, Lee?"

"Curtain rods," Oswald lied in a short, curt voice.

"Oh yeah," said Frazier, backing the car up. "You told me about them yesterday."

It was a long uncomfortable ride for Wes. Oswald had nothing to say, and they drove into the Depository's parking lot in an awkward silence. Without so much as a "thank you," Oswald got out, grabbed his package, and hurried toward the building.

"Hey, Lee," called Frazier. "Wait up!" Usually the two walked in together, but Oswald was already at the door. He didn't even pause as he hurried in, leaving Wes outside.

"What's wrong with him," wondered Frazier. It would be only hours before the young man learned the awful truth of Oswald's plan.

CHAPTER 4 — KENNEDY'S LAST STOP

Every building and street that the president would travel had to be checked out by the Secret Service. Everywhere the president went, there were police and Secret Service agents. Any person in Dallas who could possibly be a risk was checked out. Although Oswald was known to be a Communist, he had no known history of violence (he was never linked to the attempt on Maj. General Walker's life). Oswald was not considered to be a risk.

Gerald A. Behn was the special agent in charge of White House security. It was his job to keep the president and vice president and their families safe. And it wasn't an easy task. For example, President Kennedy had ordered that, unless it was raining, the bubbletop was to be left off his car so that the people of Dallas could see him, and he could wave to them. Although the top of the car wasn't bulletproof, it did offer some safety.

Also, Kennedy did not like it when the Secret Service agents ran beside his car, or jumped on the back bumpers. He knew he needed to be protected, but he didn't like to be surrounded so closely. So, for the Dallas parade, the agents were ordered to follow in the next car back. That made it much more difficult for them to do their job. How could they place themselves between the president and danger when they were in another car? But then again, it was difficult to argue with the president of the United States.

When *Air Force One* landed at Love Field, the Kennedys stepped out into Dallas sunshine and 76° weather. It would be a nice day. Pausing long enough to shake a few of the hundreds of hands that waved to them by the fence, the presidential group then got in their cars. They began their slow drive through downtown and on to Dallas' Trade Mart, where Kennedy would give a luncheon speech. With President and Mrs. Kennedy rode Governor and Mrs. Connally. It was a trip the governor almost didn't live to tell about.

CHAPTER 5 —
KILLING THE PRESIDENT

It was almost noon. Excitedly, the employees of the Depository stopped working early to eat and hurry outside to wait for the president to come by. Except for one employee. Charlie Givens called to Oswald from the elevator. "Come on, boy! It's near lunchtime."

"No, sir," said Oswald angrily. He had things to do and didn't want to be bothered. Alone on the 6th floor, Oswald took several cartons of books and moved them over to the east corner window. He built a small "fort" where he could look out without being seen from inside. Finally, he dragged a smaller box inside and sat down. Quickly, he put his rifle together and loaded it. Then he waited.

In the limo, President Kennedy smiled and waved, repeating over and over, "Thank you. Thank you." As far as the eye could see, people were lined up on the streets and sidewalks. Hundreds leaned out of buildings. It was a president's dream and a Secret Serviceman's nightmare. An ocean of smiling faces; a sea of danger.

At 12:30 p.m., the car turned onto Elm Street. Mrs. Connally turned to the president in the back seat and said, "Mr. Kennedy, you can't say that Dallas doesn't love you." Kennedy just smiled and continued waving at the crowd. They were within five minutes of the Trade Mart. The Secret Service agents were thinking that everything was going to be okay.

As the president's car drew near, Oswald stood up and balanced his rifle on yet another carton. With deadly accuracy, he placed the crosshairs of his scope on the president. For an instant, Kennedy's smiling face seemed to look directly at the killer, then it turned as he continued to wave.

Oswald fired. He missed, hitting the concrete just in back of the car. But he had learned his lesson with Maj. General Walker. He paused, as did everyone on the street as they asked themselves, "What was that?" Then Oswald fired two more shots. The first hit the president through the throat and travelled on through the next seat up, hitting Gov. Connally in the back. The second shot hit Kennedy directly on the back of the head, killing him instantly.

19

Mrs. Kennedy had only a second to ask, "What's the matter, Jack?" before the final bullet ended her husband's life. The next minutes were a blur as the limo raced to Parkland Hospital. But it was all over for the 35th President of the United States. Almost the entire right side of his brain was gone. John Kennedy was dead.

CHAPTER 6 —
OSWALD IS CAPTURED

Oswald hid his rifle among the boxes and hurried down to the second floor lunchroom. He knew that the police would be in the building in seconds. Sure enough, as Oswald stood there panting softly, his boss, Roy Truly, came up the stairs, leading Officer Marrion L. Baker through the building.

"Do you know this man?" asked Baker, pointing his gun at Oswald.

"Yes," replied Truly.

"Does he work here?"

"Yes, he works for me," said Truly impatiently.

The killer must be upstairs and he wanted him caught. The two hurried on. Oswald bought a Coca-Cola and calmly walked outside.

Already people were giving descriptions to police. Many had seen the man with a rifle standing at the 6th floor window of the Depository. Many thought he was a Secret Serviceman. Others were too excited about the president's approaching car to think anything about it. But now everyone was being asked, and the descriptions given fit the man who, unnoticed, entered a nearby bus.

Oswald returned to his rented room. He put on a jacket and placed a .38 caliber revolver in his belt. Pausing only to grab a few extra bullets, he raced out. His housekeeper, Mrs. Earlene Roberts, said, "Oh, you are in a hurry." She had never seen the young man move so fast. Odd.

Meanwhile, back at the School Book Depository, the employees had been rounded up. In a short time, it was clear who was missing: Lee Harvey Oswald. A second search of the building discovered the deadly rifle and empty bullet shells behind Oswald's fort. It was only a short while before the police knew who they were after.

Instead of leaving town, Oswald walked aimlessly through a rundown section of Dallas. He hadn't tried to escape. He could have caught a bus out of town, but didn't. Instead, he walked and waited. Suddenly, he heard the sound of Officer J.D. Tippit's police car behind him. Tippit knew the police were looking for a 25-to-30-year-old male wearing a work jacket and slacks, medium height, thin, black or possibly brown hair. The man ahead of him fit the description.

Tippit stopped beside Oswald and leaned across the seat to ask the man some questions. Not satisfied with Oswald's answers, Tippit got out and started around the car toward Oswald, reaching for his pistol. However, before the officer could get his gun out, Oswald whipped out his .38 and shot the stunned officer four times. Screams erupted on the street as several witnesses watched the horrible killing. Tippit lived only 15 seconds, muttering words no one could understand. Oswald threw the bullet shells in some bushes and raced away. Someone picked them up and called for help.

Johnny Brewer, a 23-year-old manager of a shoe store, saw a strange man ducking into doorways and keeping his head down as police cars drove by. He watched as the man moved across the street and entered the Texas Theater without paying. No customers were in his store, so Brewer went across to the theater and had the cashier call the police.

In minutes, the theater was surrounded by 16 police. Inside sat one killer and 13 movie-goers. Officer Nick McDonald walked down the aisle towards Oswald, almost as if planning to walk past him, then turned sharply and shouted, "On your feet!"

Oswald stood and raised his hands as if surrendering. "It's all over," he said. But the killer was not above trying to shoot one more man. In a second, he hit McDonald in the head and reached down for his gun. The policeman reacted instantly. McDonald punched Oswald and grabbed the gun. As they struggled, Oswald pulled the trigger, but nothing happened. There was no bullet in the chamber. Other officers joined the fight and soon had Oswald handcuffed.

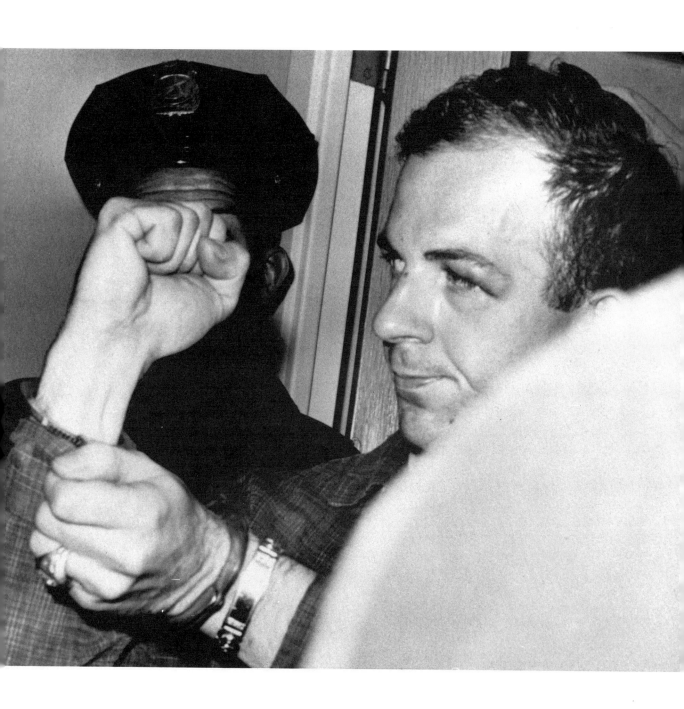

24

Struggling against his handcuffs, Oswald pleaded, "Don't hit me any more!" Then as he was dragged from the theater, he yelled, "This is police brutality!" However, the officers had no sympathy for the man who had tried to kill Officer McDonald, who they knew killed Officer Tippit, and believed had killed the president. In less than an hour and a half since the shooting, Oswald was brought to Dallas Police Headquarters.

CHAPTER 7 — MORE VIOLENCE

Oswald sat in an office at police headquarters. Detective Richard Stovall asked, "What's your name?"

"Lee Oswald."

"What's your name?" asked Detective Guy Rose again.

"Alex Hidell," answered Oswald.

It would be shown that the gun found in the Texas School Book Depository was owned by an "Alex Hidell." It would be shown that the bullets which killed Officer Tippit had come from the gun which Oswald had in the theater. It would be shown that Lee Harvey Oswald, in an effort to be remembered forever, was the murderer who ended the lives of two men on that terrifying November day in 1963.

For the next several days, the country would mourn the loss of their 46-year old leader. No one could believe he was gone. The new president, Lyndon B. Johnson, had to take over. Mrs. Kennedy had to plan a funeral, instead of birthday parties for her daughter, Caroline turning 6, and her son, John, just turning 3. Painfully, sorrowfully, the entire world cried.

In Dallas, many of the citizens were ashamed. How could this happen to their city? Jack Ruby, who owned a nightclub in town, was a strong supporter of President Kennedy. He could hardly believe that this wonderful president was gone.

Blown away by some crazy nobody with a big rifle. Coming out of his office that afternoon, Ruby decided to close his club for the next several days. He had to see this Lee Harvey Oswald for himself.

Ruby waited with a group of more than 100 reporters and photographers as Oswald was taken back and forth through police headquarters. He saw the man. He still couldn't believe it.

Ruby returned home to watch T.V., trying to understand everything that had happened. All he knew was that Oswald had killed Kennedy, and Oswald had to pay.

On Sunday, November 24, Ruby went to send a telegram at a building across from police headquarters. Since he was carrying over $2,000, he also took his revolver. As he was leaving, he noticed a crowd had gathered at police headquarters. "What's going on?" asked Ruby to someone on the street.

"They're moving Oswald," answered the stranger. "Lots of calls have come in threatening to kill him. He's going to a maximum-security cell."

Ruby waited until the policeman guarding the entrance to the basement was busy stopping traffic, then headed down to take his place among the reporters inside. Oswald stepped out, arm-in-arm with several policemen. He seemed almost happy as he walked toward the bright lights of the TV cameras. He was finally famous. However, his smiles turned to horror as Ruby stepped forward, pointed his .38 Colt Cobra revolver at Oswald's lower chest, and fired.

Oswald was rushed to the same hospital that his victim, President Kennedy, had been in only two days before. Within two hours, the killer was dead.

EPILOGUE

Jack Ruby was arrested and found guilty of killing Lee Harvey Oswald. He was sent to prison, and died there on January 3, 1967 of cancer.

After extensive surgery, Governor John Connally survived his wounds. Had he not been rushed so quickly to the hospital, he probably would have died.

Lee Harvey Oswald was found to be Kennedy's killer. He gained the fame that he so desperately wanted. No one will ever forget the man who shocked a nation. The man who destroyed a president, husband, and father. Oswald once said, "I want to give the people of the United States something to think about." Sadly, tragically, he did.

SOURCES CONSULTED

Bishop, Jim. **The Day Kennedy Was Shot**. New York: Funk & Wagnalls, 1968.

DeCurtis, Anthony. "Matters of Fact and Fiction." **Rolling Stone**, November 17, 1988.

Lattimer, John K. **Kennedy and Lincoln**. New York and London: Harcourt Brace Jovanovich, 1980.

Valenti, Jack. "Anniversary of an Assassination: Memories From a Last Motorcade." **Los Angeles Times**, November 23, 1986.

Wallechinsky, David, and Wallace, Irving. **The People's Almanac**. New York: Doubleday & Company, Inc., 1975.

Wallechinsky, David, and Wallace, Irving. **The People's Almanac #2**. New York: Doubleday & Company, Inc., 1978.

Zoglin, Richard. "What If Oswald Had Stood Trial?" **Time**, December 1, 1986.